Chemicals in Action

States of Matter

Chris Oxlade

Heinemann
LIBRARY

www.heinemann.co.uk/library
Visit our website to find out more information about **Heinemann Library** books.

To order:
 Phone 44 (0) 1865 888066
Send a fax to 44 (0) 1865 314091
Visit the Heinemann Bookshop at www.heinemann.co.uk/library to browse our catalogue and order online.

First published in Great Britain by Heinemann Library, Halley Court, Jordan Hill, Oxford OX2 8EJ, a division of Reed Educational and Professional Publishing Ltd. Heinemann is a registered trademark of Reed Educational & Professional Publishing Limited.

OXFORD MELBOURNE AUCKLAND JOHANNESBURG BLANTYRE
GABORONE IBADAN PORTSMOUTH NH (USA) CHICAGO

Designed by Tinstar Design (www.tinstar.co.uk)
Illustrations by Jeff Edwards.
Originated by Ambassador Litho Ltd.
Printed by Wing King Tong in Hong Kong.

ISBN 0 431 136041
06 05 04 03 02
10 9 8 7 6 5 4 3 2 1

British Library Cataloguing in Publication Data
Oxlade, Chris
States of matter. – (Chemicals in action)
1.Matter – Juvenile literature
I. Title
530

Acknowledgements
The Publishers would like to thank the following for permission to reproduce photographs:
Ace Photos p29, Chris Bonington p27, Mary Evans picture library p25, Robert Harding pp7, 18, 20, Science Photo Library pp4, 5, 9, 10, 11, 17, 19, 23 (R Maisonneure), 32, 36, 37, 38, Telegraph Colour Library p12, Tony Stone p24, Trevor Clifford pp13, 15, 21, 25, 31, 33, 35, 39.

Cover photograph reproduced with permission of Bruce Coleman.

The Publishers would like to thank Dr Nigel Saunders for his assistance in the preparation of this book.

Every effort has been made to contact copyright holders of any material reproduced in this book. Any omissions will be rectified in subsequent printings if notice is given to the Publisher.

Contents

Words appearing in the text in bold, **like this**, are explained in the glossary.

Chemicals in action

What's the link between rocket engines, medicine, gemstones and icebergs? The answer is that they are all solids, liquids or gases, or they use solids, liquids and gases to work. Solids, liquids and gases are called the three states of matter. Our knowledge of solids, liquids and gases is used in making chemicals, in engineering, in medicine, and in many other areas of science.

The study of solids, liquids and gases is part of the science of chemistry. Many people think of chemistry as something that scientists study by doing experiments in labs full of test tubes and flasks of bubbling liquids. This part of chemistry is very important. It is how scientists find out what substances are made of and how they make new materials – but this is only a tiny part of chemistry. Most chemistry happens away from laboratories, in factories and chemical plants. It is used to manufacture an enormous range of items, such as synthetic fibres for fabrics, drugs to treat diseases, explosives for fireworks, solvents for paints, and fertilizers for growing crops.

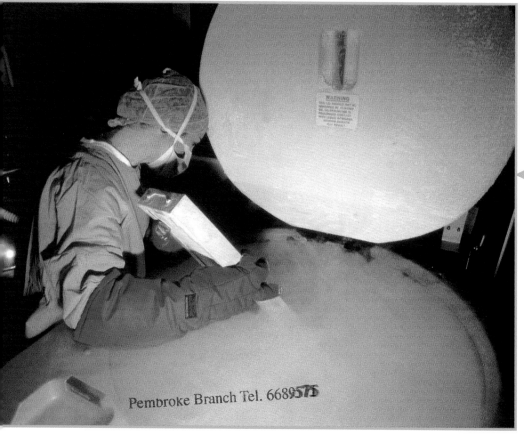

Nitrogen gas becomes a liquid below -196°C, so liquid nitrogen is used to deep-freeze medical specimens.

Pembroke Branch Tel. 6689575

*Solids often come in the form of beautiful crystals. These are crystals of the **element** sulfur.*

About the experiments

There are several experiments in the book for you to try. Doing these will help you to understand some of the chemistry in the book. An experiment is designed to help solve a scientific problem. Scientists use a logical approach to experiments so that they can conclude things from the results of the experiments. A scientist first writes down a hypothesis, which he or she thinks might be the answer to the problem, then designs an experiment to test the hypothesis. He or she then writes down the results of the experiment and concludes whether the results show that hypothesis is true or not. We only know what we do about chemistry because scientists have carefully carried out thousands of experiments over hundreds of years. Experiments have helped us to understand why different substances are solids, liquids and gases, and why they have the **properties** they do.

Doing the experiments

All the experiments in this book have been designed for you to do at home with everyday substances and equipment. They can also be done in the school laboratory. Always follow the safety advice given with each experiment, and ask an adult to help you when the instructions tell you to.

Three states of matter

All materials are solids, liquids or gases, called the three states of matter. For example, wood is a solid, water is a liquid, and the air around us is made up of different gases.

Of the thousands of different substances we have on Earth, most are solids at everyday temperatures. Only a few are gases and only a few are liquids.

Properties of solids, liquids and gases

A solid is a substance that keeps its shape – it does not flow like a liquid, or fill a space like a gas. You can't easily squash (compress), expand or change the shape of most solids, because the **particles** in them are joined firmly to each other. There are some exceptions to this rule. For example, rubber is a solid, but it can stretch and bend without breaking. There are various families of solids, such as **metals** and plastics, and solids with regular shapes, called **crystals**. The **properties** of many solids make them useful materials for manufacturing items.

A liquid is a substance that flows – it has no definite shape like a solid. It will flow to the lowest point that it can, so it always fills the bottom part of a container. Like solids, liquids are difficult to squash because their particles are closely packed together. Liquids such as oil are used in many machines.

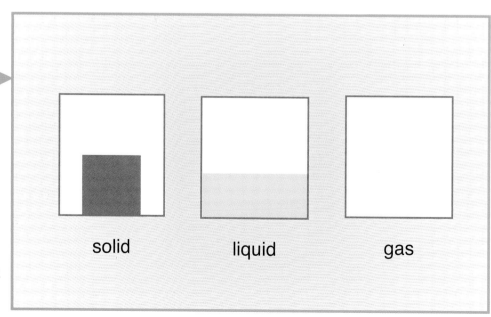

Solids, liquids and gases in containers. A solid cannot flow; a liquid flows into the bottom of a container; a gas flows to fill a container.

solid   liquid   gas

A gas is a substance that fills up the container it is in, and it flows to match the shape of the container. Gases are easy to squash. Gases and liquids are both called **fluids** because they can flow.

There is a fourth state of matter, called **plasma** that rarely exists naturally on Earth. You can find out about plasma on page 23.

Solid to liquid to gas

When we say that a substance is a solid, liquid or gas, we normally mean in everyday conditions. This is at the temperature inside a building, often called room temperature, and under normal **atmospheric pressure**. Many substances can exist in all three states of matter. The most common of these is water, and it can be a solid (ice), a liquid (water) and a gas (water vapour or steam).

A change of state happens when a substance changes from one state to another. For example, when ice melts it is going through a change of state from a solid to a liquid. These changes are normally caused by changes in temperature (for example ice melts when its temperature rises) but they can also be caused by changes in **pressure**.

Rock heated deep under the Earth's surface melts into liquid rock called **magma**. *This flows out of volcanoes as lava.*

The particle theory

Throughout this book, the properties of solids, liquids and gases, and changes of state, are explained using a **theory** called the particle theory. The particle theory is a way of thinking of substances as being made up of tiny particles that can join up with each other. These particles are **atoms** or **molecules**.

Solids

A simple definition of a solid is a substance that has a definite shape. This means that a solid object, such as this book, cannot change to become a completely different shape – it cannot flow like a liquid or a gas. A solid also has a definite **volume**; it cannot be compressed into a much smaller space, or stretched to fit into a much larger space. Most solids have high **densities**, too, which means that small solid objects feel heavy.

Inside a solid

All substances, whether they are solids, liquids or gases, are made up of tiny **particles** of matter far too small to see, even with a powerful microscope. These particles are either individual **atoms** or **molecules**. A molecule is a particle made up of two or more atoms joined to each other by links called chemical **bonds**.

In a solid each particle is joined strongly to the particles around it by chemical bonds. The bonds are like tiny springs with one end attached to each particle. This means that the particles are fixed in their positions and cannot move about. In **crystals**, the particles are arranged in regular rows and columns (see also page 14).

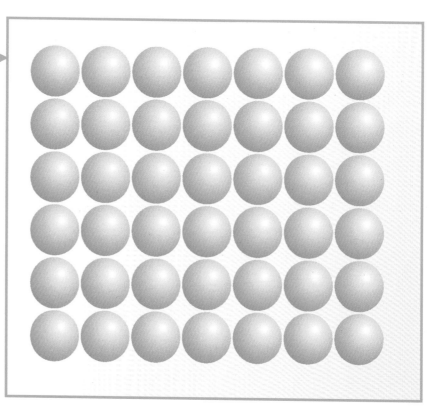

The particles in a solid are arranged in a regular pattern, and they are joined firmly to their neighbouring particles by chemical bonds.

Squashing and stretching

Particles in a solid are packed tightly together and therefore cannot be squashed or compressed easily. Most solids can be stretched a tiny bit. When they are stretched the bonds are stretched a bit so the particles are pulled slightly further apart. The particles themselves do not change size, only the bonds do. They act a bit like springs and when the force stretching them is removed they return to their original shape – and so does the solid.

If the bonds between particles are stretched too much they break. When a very brittle solid such as china is stretched, the bonds break suddenly and the china snaps. In **metals**, such as copper, the particles can move past each other without their bonds breaking, so they can be stretched into new shapes. Solids like this are described as **malleable**.

In a few solids, such as rubber, the particles are huge, curly molecules containing thousands of atoms. These solids are easy to stretch and bend because the molecules can uncurl and straighten out before they break.

The rubber in a party balloon can stretch to several times its natural size. If you stretch the rubber too far, the molecules break and separate and the balloon bursts!

Density of solids

Density is a measure of the heaviness of a substance; it is measured in grams per cubic centimetre (g/cm^3). An object made of a substance with a high density weighs more than an identical object made of a substance with lower density. The heavier the **particles** in a substance, and the closer they are packed together, the more dense the substance is. Most solids, such as iron and marble, have high densities because the particles are packed closely together. Solids that have a low density, such as wood and some plastics, are not pure solids because they have air spaces inside.

Expansion and contraction

Although the particles in a solid cannot move from place to place, they can vibrate where they are. The hotter a solid becomes, the more vigorously the particles vibrate.

As a solid is heated to a higher temperature its particles vibrate faster. The particles take up slightly more space, so the solid expands. Most solids don't expand much. For example, if a steel rail 100m long were heated so that its temperature rose by 100°C, it would only get 12cm longer. As a solid cools down, its particles vibrate more slowly and it contracts (gets smaller). You can think of the vibrating particles as being like people dancing in a packed room – the more energetically they dance, the more space they take up!

This is an expansion joint at the end of a road bridge. It has gaps that the bridge can expand into when the weather is hot.

Hard and soft solids

Some solids, such as **crystals** of bath salts, are quite soft and easy to scratch or break up. Other solids, such as diamonds, are extremely hard and very difficult to scratch or break up. Scientists use a scale of hardness to show how hard a solid is – H1 is the softest and H10 is the hardest. A **mineral** called talc has a hardness of H1, steel a hardness of H5 and diamond a hardness of H10.

The hardness of a solid depends on how its particles are arranged, and how strong the **bonds** between them are. In soft solids, like talc, the particles are joined with weak bonds. In very hard solids, like diamonds, the particles are joined to all their neighbours with strong bonds.

This is a piece of talc, the very soft mineral that has a hardness of H1.

Heat conduction

Heat energy travels through solids by a process called **conduction**. The heat is passed from one particle to the next. If you put a **metal** spoon in a hot drink, heat energy will spread up the spoon from particle to particle, gradually making the handle hot. Energy always passes from quickly vibrating, hotter particles to slowly vibrating, cooler particles – until both particles are vibrating at the same rate.

Families of solids

We can group solids with similar **properties** to each other into families, such as **metals**, ceramics, plastics, and stone. The properties of the solids in each family make the solids useful to us for different jobs.

Metals and alloys

About three-quarters of all the **elements** are metals. Metals are elements such as iron, copper and aluminium, and are all solids at room temperature – except mercury, which is a liquid. Metals are good **conductors** of heat and electricity. They are **malleable**, which means a piece of metal can be hammered into different shapes without it snapping. This would be impossible with an object made from a brittle material such as glass. Metals are also **ductile**, which means a block of metal can be gradually drawn into a long, thin wire.

Most metals are very strong. This steel framework will hold up the walls and floors of a new building.

Metals are used to make a huge range of things, from bridges and cruise ships, to tiny **electronic components**. Many of the metals we see every day in machines, furniture and objects such as coins, are **alloys**. An alloy is a mixture of different metals or a mixture of a metal with a **non-metal**. Making a metal into an alloy improves its properties for certain jobs. The most common alloy is steel, which is an alloy made up of iron with a small amount of carbon. Steel is stronger and more malleable than iron.

Plastics

Plastics are solids manufactured from chemicals **extracted** from oil, gas and plants. There is a wide range of plastics, each one suitable for a different job. For example, plastics used in casings for machines such as computers are rigid and hard, whereas plastics used for carrier bags are bendy and soft. Plastics can be made resistant to heat, which means they do not burn or go soft when heated, and resistant to chemicals which means they do not react with chemicals such as **acids**. They are also easy to shape by moulding.

Ceramics

Ceramics are materials such as pottery, china and glass. They are made from substances found in the ground, such as rock, clay and sand. For example, pottery is made by heating wet clay in a kiln, which makes the clay go hard. Ceramics are very good insulators against heat and electricity, and are resistant to chemicals. For example, strong acids are stored in glass bottles because glass does not react with acids.

Experiment: Good and bad conductors

PROBLEM: Which materials are good conductors of electricity and which are bad conductors?

HYPOTHESIS: If you put pieces of material into a simple circuit containing a battery and bulb, the bulb will only light if the material is a conductor.

> **EQUIPMENT**
> torch
> aluminium cooking foil
> sticky tape
> objects to test – made of metal, wood, plastic, ceramic etc.

Experiment steps

1 Cut a strip of aluminium foil about 1cm wide. If you want to test large objects, make your strip a long one.

2 Dismantle the torch. Use sticky tape to stick one end of the foil strip to the bottom of the battery. Wrap the other end of the foil around the side or screw thread of the bulb (do not let it touch the bottom of the bulb).

3 To test an object to see if it conducts electricity, touch the object with the top of the battery and the bottom of the bulb at the same time. If the bulb lights, the object conducts electricity well. If it doesn't light up, the object is a poor conductor of electricity.

CONCLUSION: All the metal objects tested made the light bulb glow. The other materials tested, did not. This shows that metals are good conductors of electricity and the other materials are bad conductors of electricity.

Crystals

Some solids come in the form of **crystals**. The **particles** in a crystal are arranged neatly in a regular pattern called a **crystal lattice**, with each particle attached to its neighbours. Solids that come in the form of crystals are described as crystalline; examples of everyday crystal substances are sodium chloride (common salt) and granulated sugar.

Because of the neat arrangement of their particles, many crystals have straight edges and flat faces. Different crystalline substances form crystals with different numbers of faces and edges at different angles to each other. For example, sodium chloride forms simple cubic crystals with six faces, like tiny dice.

Forming crystals

The formation of crystals is called **crystallization**. Crystals form either when a molten substance cools down to become a solid, or when a **solution** containing a substance cools or evaporates and the substance comes out of the solution. During crystallization, particles join together to make a solid crystal. If this happens slowly, large crystals are formed and if it happens quickly, smaller crystals are formed. For example igneous rocks, formed when **magma** cools slowly underground, have large crystals – but when magma cools quickly above ground the rocks formed have small crystals.

Two simple crystal shapes (cubic and hexagonal) and how the particles are arranged inside them. The shape of each crystal matches the arrangement of the particles in it.

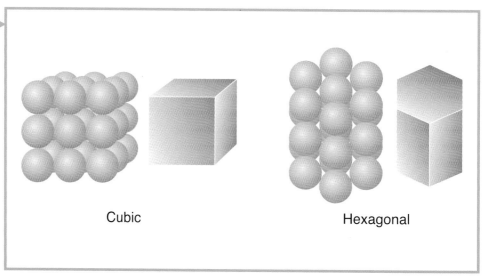

Cubic   Hexagonal

Experiment: Growing crystals

PROBLEM: How can you make crystals?

HYPOTHESIS: Crystals are often left when a liquid cools down or dries up. Cooling a solution of a substance might make crystals grow.

EQUIPMENT
alum powder
glass jars
cotton thread
cocktail stick

Experiment steps

1 Fill a glass jar with warm (but not boiling) water, then add a teaspoon of alum powder and stir the water to help the powder dissolve. Keep adding powder and stirring until no more powder will dissolve. This is called a saturated solution.

2 Allow the excess powder to settle at the bottom of the jar and then pour the solution into another jar, leaving the excess powder behind.

3 Tie a short piece of cotton thread to a cocktail stick and hang it in the solution. (You might need to put a weight on the end of the thread, to keep it inside the solution). Leave the jar where it will not be disturbed.

CONCLUSION: After a few days an alum crystal has formed on the thread. It has formed because there was more alum in the solution than the water could hold.

Liquids

A simple definition of a liquid is a substance that flows to fill the bottom of the container it is in. A liquid does not have a definite shape like a solid, but it does have a definite **volume** like a solid. This means it cannot easily be compressed into a much smaller space, or stretched into a much larger space. At room temperature, only a few **elements** and **compounds** are liquids, the most common is water (see page 20). Most other liquids, such as fruit juices, are **mixtures** made up mostly of water.

Inside a liquid

The **particles** in a liquid are attracted to each other, but they do not form permanent chemical **bonds** with each other. They are closely packed together, but they are always on the move. They are like people packed in a room moving around in little groups, but occasionally changing from one group to another.

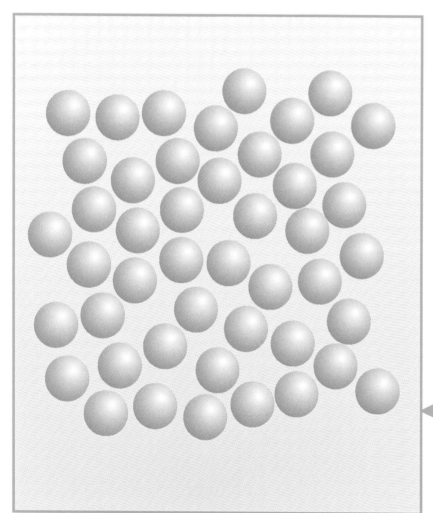

Most liquids have slightly lower **densities** than solids because their particles are not so closely packed together. Water has a density of exactly 1 g/cm³. This means that a litre of water weighs one kilogram and a cubic metre of water weighs 1000 kilograms (one tonne). Mercury is the only metal that is a liquid at room temperature. Its density is 13.6g/cm³.

The particles in a liquid are closely packed and randomly arranged, and they can move around each other.

Compressing and stretching

A liquid can change shape easily, but it cannot easily be compressed into a smaller space because its particles are closely packed together. So you cannot compress a plastic bottle full of water, but a liquid can be squashed a tiny bit more than a solid. When a liquid is squashed, the particles are squeezed closer together. If the compressing force is removed, it returns to its original volume. If you try to stretch a liquid, its particles soon break apart, so the liquid breaks up into droplets. That's why a thin stream of water from a tap breaks up into droplets.

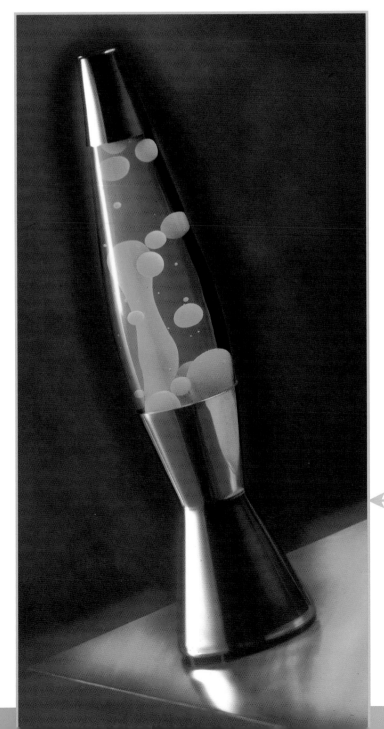

Expansion and contraction of liquids

Inside a liquid, the particles are constantly moving about. The hotter the liquid, the faster the particles move. If a liquid is heated to a higher temperature, its particles move faster than before. This makes them collide with each other more often, and so they take up more space. In turn this makes the liquid expand slightly.

Liquid at the bottom of a lava lamp gets warmed, expands, and rises to the top. At the top of the lamp the liquid cools, contracts and sinks back to the bottom of the lamp.

Liquids on the move

How easily a liquid flows is called its viscosity. Some liquids, such as water, have low viscosity and they flow easily out of a jar if you tip the jar up. Other liquids, such as cooking oil and treacle, have high viscosity and they flow slowly out of a container. Liquids made up of long **molecules**, such as oil, are very viscous because the molecules tangle with each other.

Convection currents

Liquids are not good **conductors** of heat, as the experiment on page 21 illustrates. However, heat can travel through a liquid by a process called **convection**. If one part of a liquid is heated, it expands slightly and floats upwards and is replaced by cooler liquid, which in turn is heated. The currents created in the liquids are called **convection currents**.

Diffusion in liquids

Liquids can mix naturally with each other in a process called **diffusion**. For example, if you put a drop of food colouring in some water, the colour eventually spreads completely through the water. It happens because the **particles** in a liquid are always on the move. Diffusion happens slowly because the particles keep colliding with each other.

Liquid pressure

A liquid will press on any object that is in it. This pressing is called liquid **pressure**, and the deeper down into the liquid, the greater the pressure gets. Submarines need very strong hulls to prevent being crushed by the water pressure when they are in very deep seas.

The arm of this hydraulic digger is moved by liquid that is pumped into the arm through pipes.

Blaise Pascal (1623–1662)

French mathematician and physicist Blaise Pascal studied pressure in liquids and gases. He was the first person to realize that liquids press in all directions on objects, not just downwards. This is known as Pascal's principle. He went on to invent the hydraulic press and also the first mechanical calculating machine.

Experiment: Convection currents

PROBLEM: How can you see convection currents?

HYPOTHESIS: By adding some coloured dye to water and heating the water, the convection currents may be visible.

EQUIPMENT
large glass jar
dish
food colouring

Experiment steps

1 Fill the glass jar with cold water, then stand it in a dish and leave it for ten minutes so that movements in the water settle down.

2 Pour some hot water into the dish. Carefully put several drops of food colouring into the water in the jar. Watch what happens to it.

CONCLUSION: The colour moves up and down the jar, showing that warm water is flowing up the jar and is being replaced by cool water from above.

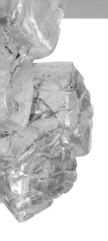

Water

Water is a tasteless, colourless liquid. It is the most common liquid on Earth and is vital for animals and plants to live. It is also the only substance that we regularly see in all its three states, which are ice, liquid water and water **vapour**. The **particles** that make up water are **molecules**, each containing two hydrogen **atoms** and one oxygen atom. The chemical formula for water is H_2O.

Ice

Ice is the solid form of water, and it is peculiar because it is less **dense** than liquid water – most substances become more dense when they turn from liquid to solid. This is why ice floats on the top of water. On a frozen lake, the layer of ice acts like a blanket, stopping the water underneath from freezing too. Under the ice, life goes on as normal for fish and other aquatic animals.

Water vapour

The gaseous form of water is called water vapour. There is always some water vapour in the air, but you cannot see it. You can only tell that it is there because when it hits a cold surface, such as a window, it cools and turns into small droplets of liquid water. The word steam is sometimes used instead of water vapour, and it is also used to describe the clouds that come out of a hot kettle or pan. Steam is actually made up of water droplets that form as the water vapour leaves the kettle spout and cools to become a liquid again.

Ice is only slightly less dense than water, so most of this iceberg is hidden under the water.

Water is a poor conductor

1 This boiling tube contains 5cm of water with some wire/steel wool pushed into the bottom and an ice cube placed on top of this. The wire wool reduces convection currents going up and down the tube, but still allows heat to travel through the water by **conduction**.

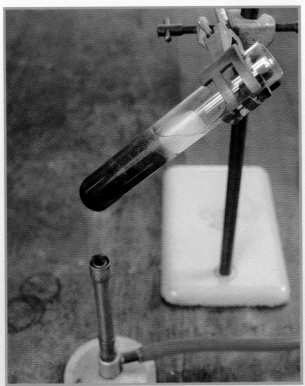

2 When the end of the boiling tube is heated, until the water boils, the ice does not melt. This is because the heat does not travel through the water. Water is a poor conductor of heat.

Gases

A simple definition of a gas is a substance that expands to fill the container it is in. A gas does not have a definite shape, which means that it can flow and change shape like a liquid. Neither does it have a definite **volume**, which means that it can be compressed into a much smaller space and also that it expands when it is allowed to.

Inside a gas

The **particles** in a gas are **atoms** or **molecules**; they are whizzing about at high speed, bouncing off anything they hit, and each other if they collide. They are not attached to each other in any way. You can think of the particles as being like people running about in a room, bouncing off the walls and each other! You could make the room smaller or bigger and the people, the 'gas', would still fill it.

Gases have **densities** thousands of times lower than solids and liquids because of the spaces between their particles. The density of a gas goes up if the gas is squeezed into a smaller volume and goes down if it expands to fill a larger volume.

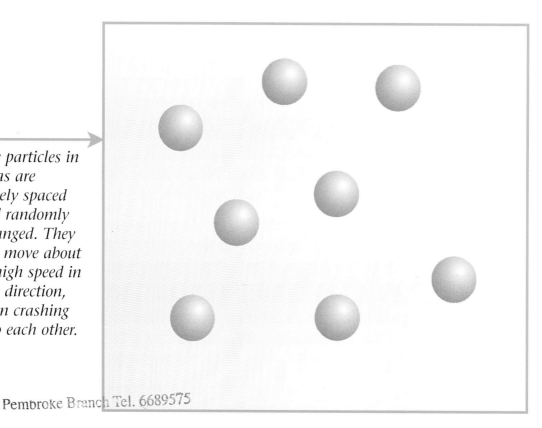

The particles in a gas are widely spaced and randomly arranged. They can move about at high speed in any direction, often crashing into each other.

Common gases

The most common gases on Earth are found in the air that makes up the Earth's **atmosphere**. They include nitrogen and oxygen. You can find out more about the air on page 26. Other gases such as hydrogen and ammonia are used for the production of chemicals, such as fertilizers, and they are made in **chemical plants**. Natural gas, used for cooking and heating, is a **fossil fuel** mostly made up of methane.

Diffusion in gases

Like liquids, gases can also spread and mix with each other by **diffusion**. You can smell the food on other people's plates because the gases given off by the food diffuse through the air to your nose. Diffusion is faster in gases than it is in liquids because the particles in a gas are whizzing about, but it is still quite a slow process because the particles in the gas keep hitting each other and changing direction.

Plasma

You may be interested to know that there is another state of matter, called plasma. It only exists at extremely high temperatures or very low **pressures**. It is formed when the **electrons** in the atoms that make up a gas become separated from their **nuclei**. Plasma has different **properties** from a gas; for example, a plasma is a good **conductor** of electricity. On Earth, air is changed to plasma during a lightning strike and there is plasma inside a working fluorescent lamp.

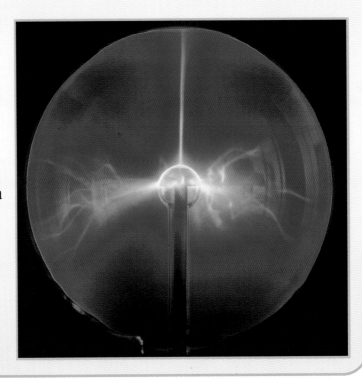

Gas pressure

The **particles** of a gas bounce off any object they hit. In fact millions of gas particles bounce off you every second. They also bounce off the sides of any container the gas is in. These collisions create a push on the surface of objects called gas **pressure**. The more frequent the collision and the faster the particles are moving, the higher the gas pressure is.

Increasing gas pressure

Changing the temperature or **volume** of a gas changes its pressure. Imagine a container full of gas: if the gas is heated its particles move faster. This makes them hit the sides of the container harder and more often, so the gas pressure increases. Now imagine a syringe full of gas: if the plunger is pushed in to decrease the volume of the gas, the particles in the gas have a smaller space to move in. They hit the sides of the container more often, increasing the gas pressure.

Gases and heat

Gases are poor conductors of heat. Energy cannot be passed from one particle to the next because the particles are not closely packed. This is why gases are used in insulating materials. For example, a duvet traps pockets of air that stop heat escaping from your body. Heat can move through a gas by **convection**, as it does through liquids.

Pressurized air makes this road drill work. Machines that use gas to work are called 'pneumatic' machines.

Jacques Charles (1746–1823)

Frenchman Jacques Charles was a government official, teacher and physicist. He is famous for his experiments with gases, and in 1787 he discovered that gases expand at the same rate when they are heated. This is the basis for Charles' Law, which states that the volume of a gas is proportional to the temperature. Charles also made the first flight in a hydrogen-filled balloon, in 1783.

Experiment: Expansion and contraction of air

PROBLEM: What happens to the volume of air when it is heated and cooled?

HYPOTHESIS: Trapping some air in a balloon, then changing the temperature while measuring the size of the balloon, will show if the air changes in volume.

EQUIPMENT
party balloon
balloon pump
sticky tape

Experiment steps

1 Use the pump to inflate a party balloon to a size that will just fit in your freezer, then carefully stick a length of sticky tape around the outside of the balloon.

2 Put the balloon in the freezer for a few minutes and then look at the sticky tape. What has happened to the air in the balloon?

3 Remove the balloon from the freezer so that it warms up again. Watch again what happens to the sticky tape.

CONCLUSION: The sticky tape wrinkles when the balloon is cooled. This shows that air contracts when it is cooled, and it expands again when it heats up.

Air and the atmosphere

Air makes up a blanket of gas around the Earth called the **atmosphere**. Air is actually a **mixture** of several different gases, and it is colourless, tasteless and odourless (does not smell). The gases in it are vital for life and take part in chemical reactions such as burning.

Gases of the air

Ninety-nine per cent of the air is made up of nitrogen (78 per cent) and oxygen (21 per cent); the remaining 1 per cent is mainly argon, from the group of gases called the noble gases.

Animals and plants need oxygen, which they take from the air for **respiration**. There is normally some water **vapour** in the air as well, and on very humid days it can make up more than four per cent of the air. This water vapour comes from water on the Earth's surface that **evaporates** in the Sun. It plays an important part in the water cycle because it allows water to be transported through the atmosphere.

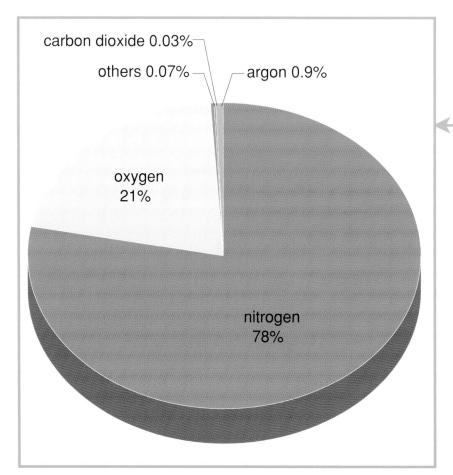

carbon dioxide 0.03%

others 0.07%

argon 0.9%

oxygen
21%

nitrogen
78%

A pie chart of the gases that make up the air in the lower atmosphere of the Earth. It shows that nitrogen and oxygen make up 99 per cent of the air.

The air gets thinner as you move up through the atmosphere. Mountaineers often need extra oxygen to breathe at high altitude so they have to carry oxygen in tanks.

Carbon dioxide makes up just 0.03 per cent of the air, but is needed by plants for **photosynthesis**. It is also the main 'greenhouse' gas. Greenhouse gases trap heat from the Sun in the atmosphere, in a similar way to how glass traps heat in a greenhouse. Without this 'greenhouse effect', the Earth would be a freezing, lifeless planet.

However, increasing amounts of carbon dioxide in the atmosphere, created by the burning of **fossil fuels**, are making the atmosphere become warmer – this 'enhanced greenhouse effect' is causing **global warming**. The air also contains other polluting gases made by burning fuels, such as sulfur dioxide – which causes **acid** rain.

The ozone layer

Ozone is a gas that is a form of oxygen. Each **molecule** of ozone contains three oxygen **atoms** instead of two, as in normal oxygen molecules, and its formula is O_3. The ozone layer is a layer of the atmosphere about 25 kilometres above the Earth's atmosphere. The high concentration of ozone there reduces the amount of harmful rays from the Sun reaching the Earth's surface.

Changes of state

A change of state happens when a substance changes from being in one state of matter to being in another state. For example, when ice (the solid form of water) changes to liquid water, the water is said to change state. Changes of state normally happen when the temperature of a substance changes. As the temperature increases, substances change from solid to liquid and then from liquid to gas. As the temperature decreases, they change from gas to liquid and then from liquid to solid. A substance always goes through changes of state at the same temperature. For example, pure water always changes from ice to liquid water at 0°C.

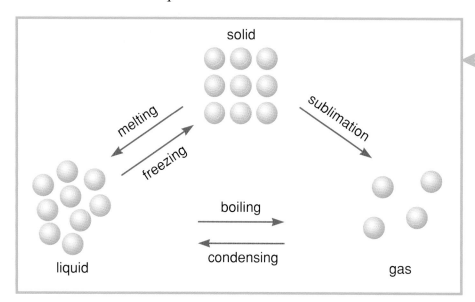

The triangle of changes of state from solid to liquid to gas and back again. Sublimation is the change of state from a solid straight back to a gas.

Physical and reversible changes

Changes of state are physical changes. This means that when a substance changes state only its physical **properties** change. Its chemical make-up stays the same. Changes of state are also reversible changes. This means that if a substance changes state it can change back again. For example, if a solid piece of metal is heated until it melts, it will always turn back to a solid when it cools again.

Not all substances can exist in different states. For example, if wood is heated it never melts, instead when it gets hot enough it burns. Burning wood is an example of a chemical change, because it creates a new substance. It is also a permanent change because the wood cannot be got back once burnt.

Melting and freezing

Melting is the change of state from solid to liquid. The temperature at which this change happens is called a substance's melting point. The melting point of ice is 0 °C and the melting point of iron is 1535 °C.

Freezing is the change of state from liquid to solid. It is the opposite of melting, and happens at the melting point as a substance cools.

Boiling and condensation

Boiling is the change of state from liquid to gas, and it is the opposite of **condensing**. A substance's boiling point is the temperature at which it changes from liquid to gas. The boiling point of water is 100°C and the boiling point of iron is 2861°C.

Condensation is the change of state from a gas to a liquid, and it happens at the boiling point as the substance cools.

Winter ice in rivers and lakes turns back to water when temperatures rise above 0°C when spring arrives.

Changes of state and particles

Changes of state happen when the **particles** in solids, liquids and gases either break away from each other or join up with each other. Here's what happens during each change of state.

When a solid is heated, its particles vibrate more and more. When it reaches a certain temperature (called its melting point), some of the **bonds** between the particles begin to break. This allows the particles to break free from their positions and begin to move about. When this happens the solid has melted to become a liquid. If a liquid cools, its particles slow down. Eventually the bonds will form again, and it will become a solid again.

When a liquid is heated, its particles move about faster and faster. When it reaches a certain temperature (called its boiling point), the particles break free from each other completely. The liquid has boiled to become a gas. If a gas cools, its particles slow down. Eventually bonds will begin to form again, and the gas will **condense** to become a liquid.

Water vapour has cooled and condensed to form droplets of liquid water on this window. We often call these droplets condensation, but in science condensation means turning from a gas to a liquid.

Evaporation

Evaporation is also a change of state from liquid to gas, but it happens when the temperature of a liquid is below its boiling point. In a liquid, particles moving near the surface sometimes escape from the surface of the liquid, forming a gas above the liquid. This process is called evaporation. Puddles gradually dry up because of evaporation.

Changing volumes

Most substances increase in **volume** slightly when they melt because the particles in liquid are slightly further apart than they are in a solid. Water is an exception to the rule because ice is slightly less **dense** than water. All substances increase greatly in volume when they boil because particles in a gas are widely spread.

What state?

You can predict what state a substance will be in at a certain temperature by looking at a table of melting and boiling points. For example, the metal mercury has a melting point of -39°C, and a boiling point of 357°C, so at room temperature (about 20 °C) it is a liquid. In extremely cold weather it would be a solid and in a very hot oven it would be a gas.

Changing melting and boiling points

If conditions stay the same, the melting and boiling points of a substance stay the same too. The melting point and boiling point will change if the substance is not pure, or if the air **pressure** around it changes. For example, the **freezing point** of salty water is a few degrees below 0°C. On top of high mountains, where the air pressure is lower, the boiling point of water is several degrees below 100°C.

Materials that are mixtures, like chocolate for example, tend to go soft and melt gradually rather than melting at an exact temperature.

Energy for changes

We know that substances have to be heated to raise their temperature to melting or boiling point. Once they have reached their melting or boiling point, more heating does not make them hotter, it makes them change state instead. The heating provides the energy that is needed to break the **bonds** between the **particles**.

Even metals melt, given enough heat.

For example, water heated in a kettle gets hotter until its temperature reaches its boiling point of 100°C, then the water boils to make water **vapour**. Its temperature stays at 100°C because the energy from the kettle's heating element is used to turn the water to water vapour.

Cooling down

Changes of state are used to cool things down. For example, putting ice in a drink cools the drink down because the energy needed to melt the ice comes from the drink. In a similar way, sweating when it is hot cools you down because heat energy from your skin is used up when the sweat **evaporates** from your skin.

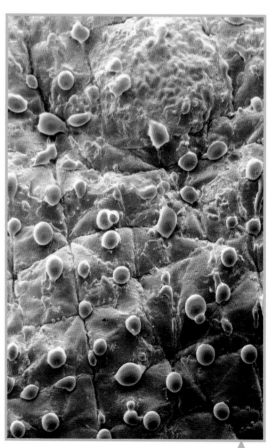

Beads of sweat on skin. They gradually evaporate, using up heat energy in your skin.

Experiment: Temperature changes

PROBLEM: What happens to the temperature of a substance as it changes state?

HYPOTHESIS: Heating a substance gently will add heat to it at a constant rate. Measuring its temperature will show what happens as the substance gets hotter and changes state.

EQUIPMENT
pan
wooden spoon
cooking thermometer (with range between 0°C and more than 100°C)
clock or watch

Experiment steps

1 Wrap some ice cubes in an old tea towel. Crush the ice cubes by standing on them or asking an adult to hit them gently with a hammer. Put the ice in a pan, add a small amount of cold water and stir. Use the thermometer to measure the temperature of the mixture and write it down.

2 Ask an adult to put the pan on the stove, then heat it gently and stir with a wooden spoon. Measure the temperature every minute and write it down.

3 When the water has been boiling for a minute, turn the heat off. Do not let the pan boil dry.

4 Draw a graph with time along the horizontal axis and temperature along the vertical axis. Plot the temperature for each minute.

CONCLUSION: At the start of the experiment all the heat goes into melting the ice – so the temperature stays at 0°C. Once the ice has melted, the heat is used to increase the temperature of the liquid. At the end, all the heat goes into boiling the water to make water vapour.

The water cycle

Towering dark clouds, pouring rain and fast-flowing rivers are all evidence of the Earth's water on the move. The water circulates between the oceans and seas, the **atmosphere**, the land and the rivers. This circulation is called the water cycle. It happens as water changes state from liquid water to water **vapour** and back again, and as water vapour is carried along in the atmosphere. If these changes of state did not happen, water would never get onto the land, so animals and plants could not live there.

Water in the air

Water is constantly **evaporating** from the world's oceans, seas, lakes and land, into the air above. Moving air carries the water vapour away and as this damp air rises higher in the atmosphere it cools. This makes some of the water vapour turn back to liquid water, which forms tiny droplets we see as clouds. If the droplets get big enough they fall to the ground as rain or snow, which soaks into the ground or runs off into streams and rivers. The water eventually returns to the sea.

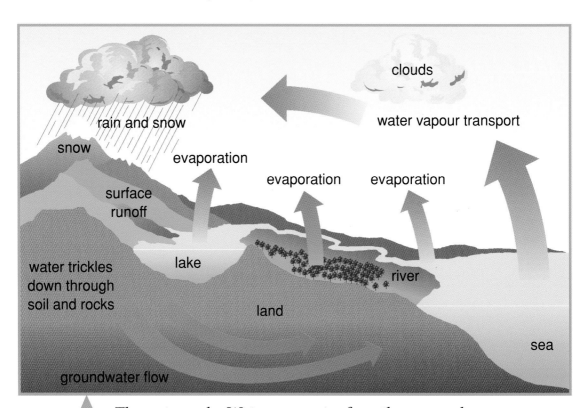

The water cycle. Water evaporates from the seas and land into the air, condenses to form clouds, falls as rain and snow, soaks into the ground or runs back into the sea along rivers.

Experiment: A water cycle model

PROBLEM: How does the water cycle work?

HYPOTHESIS: Making a simple model will show how water travels around in the water cycle.

Experiment steps

EQUIPMENT
large rectangular cardboard box, such as a
    shoe box
clear plastic food wrap
thin cardboard cut from a cereal packet
sticky tape
glass dish

1 Put the dish in one end of the box. Cut some cardboard into a rectangular shape, and fold it down the middle into a V shape (shiny printed side up). Tape the cardboard channel into the other end of the box so that any water flowing down the V will drip into the dish. This is your 'river' channel.

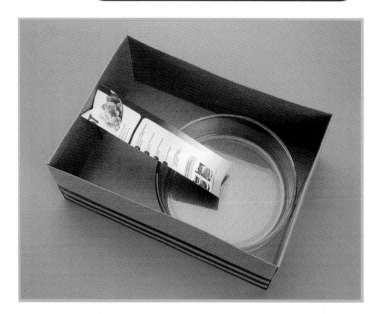

2 Pour some hot water into the dish. Cover the top of the box with clear food wrap. Put some ice on the wrap above the cardboard channel.

3 Watch what happens under the ice and in the channel.

CONCLUSION: Water evaporates from the dish (a model of the sea) and the water vapour spreads through the box. When it hits the cold wrap under the ice it **condenses** (forming model clouds), the 'rainwater' then drips onto the channel and runs back into the dish.

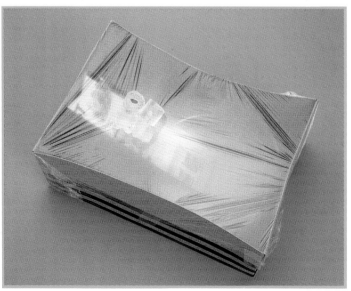

Mixtures

A **mixture** is a substance that contains different **elements** and **compounds** that are not joined together by chemical **bonds**. For example, air is a mixture; it contains some elements, such as oxygen and nitrogen, and some compounds, such as carbon dioxide (a compound of carbon and oxygen). Some mixtures contain just solids, just liquids or just gases, but some are mixtures of substances in two or three different states. Some mixtures are **solutions**, formed when a solid (called the **solute**) dissolves in a liquid (called the **solvent**).

Separating mixtures

Chemists often need to separate mixtures into their different constituents. For example, they might need to extract a useful chemical from a mixture, remove the impurities from a substance to purify it, or find out what substances are in a mixture.

To separate mixtures, chemists make use of the fact that the different elements and compounds in the mixture have different **properties**, such as different boiling points or **densities**. There are four main ways of separating mixtures – **filtration**, **evaporation**, **distillation** and **chromatography**.

These building panels contain solid foam, a mixture containing plastic and gas.

Evaporation

Evaporation is a method of getting a dissolved solid from a solution. For example, you could use evaporation to **extract** the salt from salty water. The salty solution is put into a wide container so that a large area of solution is in contact with the air. The solvent (the water) gradually evaporates (in the same way that a puddle dries up) and is lost into the air. The **particles** of the solid (the salt) do not evaporate, so eventually only the solid is left in the container.

Distillation

Distillation is a method of getting a solvent from a solution. For example, you would use distillation if you wanted to retrieve the water from salty water. The solution is put in a closed flask and heated until the solvent boils to make a gas. The gas flows along a tube into a separate container where it cools and **condenses** back into liquid, and the solute is left in the flask.

Fractional distillation is used to separate a mixture of liquids that have different boiling points. The mixture is put in a closed flask and gradually heated. Each liquid in the mixture boils at a different temperature to make a gas, and the different gases are collected and condensed to turn them back into liquids.

A chemical plant where fractional distillation is used to separate the mixture of compounds in crude oil.

Filtration

Filtration is used to separate a mixture of a liquid and a solid that has not dissolved. The mixture is poured through filter paper, which has microscopic holes in it. The liquid can get through the holes but the solids cannot. For example, if you filter muddy water, the water **molecules** pass through the holes in the paper but the **particles** of soil are trapped, and the clean water can then be collected in a beaker.

Chromatography

Chromatography is used to find out the constituents (different parts) of a mixture. Scientists use it to test whether substances are pure or to find whether two mixtures contain the same constituents. The simplest type of chromatography is paper chromatography. A blob of a mixture, such as an ink (which is a mixture of dyes), is put on a piece of filter paper. The end of the paper is then placed in a **solvent**, such as water, that dissolves the mixture. The solvent moves through the paper, carrying the dissolved dyes with it. Different dyes are carried different distances before they are left on the paper.

Water is the most common solvent, but it is not the only one we can use. Other solvents such as trichloroethane are used to dissolve substances that don't dissolve in water. For example, propanone is used to dissolve nail varnish, trichloroethane dissolves grease, and white spirit dissolves gloss paint.

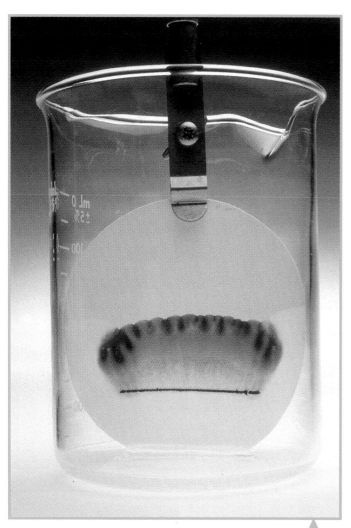

Paper chromatography being used to separate the different chemicals in a sample of ink.

Experiment: Filtering muddy water

PROBLEM: How can you clean muddy water?

HYPOTHESIS: Mud is made up of tiny particles of rock, and pouring muddy water through a filter paper should remove these particles.

Experiment steps

1 Half fill a glass jar with water and stir in some soil. The soil particles will not dissolve, so will stay solid.

2 Fold a piece of kitchen paper into a filter funnel and stand it inside the strainer over the bowl.

3 Pour the muddy water slowly into the kitchen paper, giving time for the water to drain through.

4 Carefully open out the kitchen paper.

CONCLUSION: The kitchen paper collects the solid soil particles but allows the water molecules to pass through. So the soil and water are separated.

The periodic table

The periodic table is a chart of all the known **elements**. The elements are arranged in order of their atomic numbers, but in rows, so that elements with similar **properties** are underneath each other. The periodic table gets its name from the fact that the properties the elements have repeat themselves every few elements, or periodically. The position of an element in the periodic table gives an idea of what its properties are likely to be.

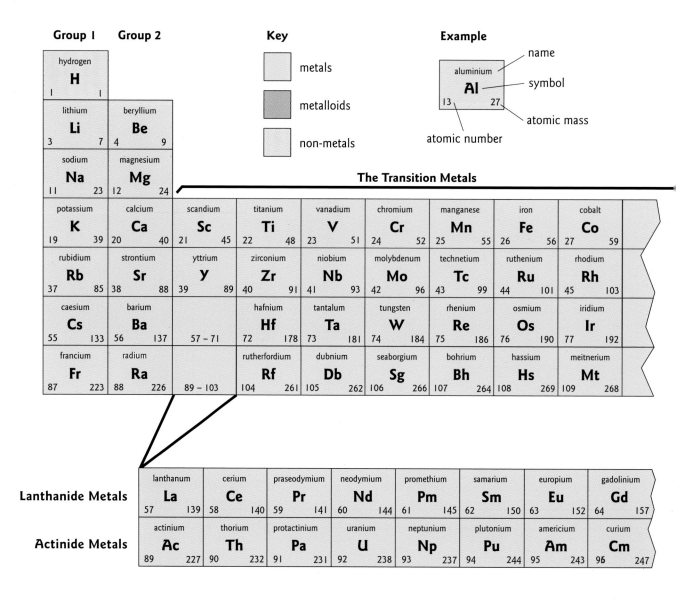

Groups and periods

The vertical columns of elements are called groups. The horizontal rows of elements are called periods. Some groups have special names:

Group 1: Alkali **metals**

Group 2: Alkaline earth metals

Group 7: Halogens

Group 0: Noble gases

The table is divided into two main sections, the metals and **non-metals**. Between the two are elements that have some properties of metals and some of non-metals. They are called semi-metals or metalloids.

Group 3	Group 4	Group 5	Group 6	Group 7	Group 0
					helium **He** 2 · 4
boron **B** 5 · 11	carbon **C** 6 · 12	nitrogen **N** 7 · 14	oxygen **O** 8 · 16	fluorine **F** 9 · 19	neon **Ne** 10 · 20
aluminium **Al** 13 · 27	silicon **Si** 14 · 28	phosphorus **P** 15 · 31	sulfur **S** 16 · 32	chlorine **Cl** 17 · 35	argon **Ar** 18 · 40

			Group 3	Group 4	Group 5	Group 6	Group 7	Group 0
nickel **Ni** 28 · 59	copper **Cu** 29 · 64	zinc **Zn** 30 · 65	gallium **Ga** 31 · 70	germanium **Ge** 32 · 73	arsenic **As** 33 · 75	selenium **Se** 34 · 79	bromine **Br** 35 · 80	krypton **Kr** 36 · 84
palladium **Pd** 46 · 106	silver **Ag** 47 · 108	cadmium **Cd** 48 · 112	indium **In** 49 · 115	tin **Sn** 50 · 119	antimony **Sb** 51 · 122	tellurium **Te** 52 · 128	iodine **I** 53 · 127	xenon **Xe** 54 · 131
platinum **Pt** 78 · 195	gold **Au** 79 · 197	mercury **Hg** 80 · 201	thallium **Tl** 81 · 204	lead **Pb** 82 · 207	bismuth **Bi** 83 · 209	polonium **Po** 84 · 209	astatine **At** 85 · 210	radon **Rn** 86 · 222
ununnilium **Uun** 110 · 271	unununium **Uuu** 111 · 272	ununbium **Uub** 112 · 285		ununquadium **Uuq** 114 · 289				

terbium **Tb** 65 · 159	dysprosium **Dy** 66 · 163	holmium **Ho** 67 · 165	erbium **Er** 68 · 167	thulium **Tm** 69 · 169	ytterbium **Yb** 70 · 173	lutetium **Lu** 71 · 175
berkelium **Bk** 97 · 247	californium **Cf** 98 · 251	einsteinium **Es** 99 · 252	fermium **Fm** 100 · 257	mendelevium **Md** 101 · 258	nobelium **No** 102 · 259	lawrencium **Lr** 103 · 262

Common elements

Here is a table of the most common **elements** from the periodic table that you may come across at home or in the laboratory. The table indicates whether the element is a solid, liquid or gas at room temperature, along with its melting and boiling points. (Melting and boiling points are for pure chemicals).

Element	Symbol	State at room temperature	Melting pt (°C)	Boiling pt (°C)
hydrogen	H	gas	-259	-253
helium	He	gas	-272	-269
lithium	Li	solid	180	1342
carbon	C	solid	3730	4830
nitrogen	N	gas	-210	-196
oxygen	O	gas	-218	-183
fluorine	F	gas	-220	-188
neon	Ne	gas	-249	-246
sodium	Na	solid	98	883
magnesium	Mg	solid	650	1090
aluminium	Al	solid	660	2519
silicon	Si	solid	1414	2900
phosphorus	P	solid	44 (white)	280
sulfur	S	solid	113	444
chlorine	Cl	gas	-101	-34
argon	Ar	gas	-189	-186
potassium	K	solid	63	759
calcium	Ca	solid	842	1487
iron	Fe	solid	1535	2861
copper	Cu	solid	1083	2595
zinc	Zn	solid	420	907
bromine	Br	liquid	-7	59
silver	Ag	solid	961	2210
tin	Sn	solid	232	2270
iodine	I	solid	114	184
gold	Au	solid	1063	2970
mercury	Hg	liquid	-39	357
lead	Pb	solid	327	1744

Common chemicals

Here is a table of some common chemicals that you may come across at home or in the laboratory. The right hand column shows their formulae.

Gases

hydrogen ....H_2

oxygen ....O_2

chlorine..Cl_2

nitrogen ....N_2

carbon dioxide ....CO_2

nitrogen dioxide ....NO_2

Liquids and solutions

water ....H_2O

hydrochloric acid..HCl

sulfuric acid..H_2SO_4

nitric acid ....HNO_3

sodium hydroxide..$NaOH$

Solids

sodium chloride ....$NaCl$

magnesium oxide..MgO

calcium carbonate..$CaCO_3$

copper sulfate ....$CuSO_4$

Glossary of technical terms

acid liquid that can eat away metals and is neutralized by alkalis and bases. Acids have a pH below 7.

alloy material made by mixing a metal with another metal or a small amount of a non-metal. For example, steel is an alloy of iron and carbon.

atmosphere layer of air that surrounds the Earth

atmospheric pressure force that the air in the Earth's atmosphere applies to all the objects in it

atom extremely tiny particle of matter. The smallest particle of an element that can exist, and which has the properties of that element. All substances are made up of atoms.

bond chemical join or connection between two atoms, ions or molecules

chemical plant place where chemicals are manufactured

chromatography method for separating different solutes that are dissolved in the same solvent, such as the dyes in ink

compound substance that contains two or more different elements joined together by chemical bonds

condensing change of state from a gas to a liquid

conduction when electricity or heat passes through a substance called a conductor

convection when heat moves from place to place in a moving gas or liquid

convection current movement that carries heat through a gas or liquid when one part of gas or liquid is heated

crystal piece of a substance that has flat sides and straight edges. Particles in a crystal are arranged in a regular pattern.

crystal lattice regular arrangement of particles inside a crystal

crystallization process of a crystal forming

density amount of a substance (or mass) in a certain volume. Density is measured in grams per cubic centimetre or kilograms per cubic metre.

diffusion movement of particles through a liquid or gas caused by the random movement of the particles

distillation method of separating a solution into its solvent and its solute, or of separating a mixture of liquids with different boiling points

ductile describes a material that can be pulled into a thin wire without breaking. Metals are ductile.

electron extremely tiny particle that is part of an atom. Electrons move around the nucleus of an atom.

electronic component device such as a capacitor or transistor in an electronic circuit

element substance that contains just one type of atom. An element cannot be changed into simpler substances.

evaporation change of state from liquid to gas when the liquid is at a temperature below its boiling point

extract remove a substance from a mixture of substances

filtration method of separating a mixture of a liquid and small particles of a solid

fluid substance that flows, such as a liquid or a gas

fossil fuel fuel formed from the remains of ancient plants and animals. Coal, oil and gas are fossil fuels.

freezing point temperature at which a substance changes state from liquid to solid as it cools down

global warming gradual warming of the Earth's atmosphere, probably caused by the burning of fossil fuels

magma molten rock under the Earth's crust

malleable describes a material that can be hammered into shape without breaking. All metals are malleable.

metal any element in the periodic table that is shiny, and that conducts electricity and heat well. Most metals are also hard.

mineral any chemical that occurs naturally in the rocks of the Earth's crust

mixture substance made up of two or more elements or compounds that are not joined together by chemical bonds

molecule type of particle. A molecule is made up of two or more atoms joined together by chemical bonds. The atoms can be of the same element or different elements.

non-metal any element in the periodic table that is not a metal. Most non-metals are gases.

nuclei central part of an atom, made up of protons and neutrons

particle very tiny piece of a substance, such as a single atom, ion, or molecule

photosynthesis chemical reaction in green plants that makes food. In photosynthesis, carbon dioxide and water react together using energy from sunlight to make sugar and oxygen.

plasma state of matter, similar to a gas, that only exists at very high temperatures or very low pressures

pressure force pushing on a certain area

properties characteristics of a substance, such as its strength, melting point and density

respiration chemical reaction that happens in all living cells. In respiration, sugar reacts with oxygen to produce carbon dioxide and water, and energy is released for our cells to use.

solute substance that dissolves in a solvent to make a solution

solution substance made when a solid, gas or liquid dissolves in a liquid. The substance that dissolves is called the solute and the liquid it dissolves in is called the solvent.

solvent liquid that a substance dissolves in to make a solution

theory ideas about how something, for example science, works

vapour the gas form of a substance that exists below the substance's boiling point

volume space that something takes up

Further reading

Chemical Chaos (Horrible Science)
Nick Arnold, Tony de Saulles, Scholastic Hippo, 1997

Chemicals in Action
Ann Fullick, Heinemann Library, 1999

Co-ordinated Science, Chemistry Foundation
Andy Bethell, John Dexter, Mike Griffths, Heinemann, 2001

The Dorling Kindersley Science Encyclopedia
Dorling Kindersley, 1993

How Science Works
Judith Hann, Dorling Kindersley, 1991

The Usborne Illustrated Dictionary of Chemistry
Jane Wertheim, Chris Oxlade and Dr. John Waterhouse
Usborne, 1987

Useful websites

http://www.heinemannexplore.com
An exciting new online resource for school libraries and
classrooms containing articles, investigations, biographies and
activities related to all areas of the science curriculum.

http://www.creative-chemistry.org.uk
An interactive chemistry site including fun practical activities,
worksheets, quizzes, puzzles and more! With links to many
more useful and interesting sites including:

http://www.bbc.co.uk/science
Loads of information on all areas of science. Includes news,
activities, games and quizzes.

http://www.chemicool.com
All you ever needed to know about the elements – and more!

http://www.webelements.com/webelements/scholar
The Periodic table – online! Discover more about all the
elements and their properties.

http://particleadventure.org
An interactive site, explaining the fundamentals of matter and
forces!

Disclaimer

All the Internet addresses (URLs) given in this book were valid at the time of going
to press. However, due to the dynamic nature of the Internet, some addresses may
have changed, or sites may have ceased to exist since publication. While the author
and publishers regret any inconvenience this may cause readers, no responsibility
for any such changes can be accepted by either the author or the publishers.

Index

Titles in the *Chemicals in Action* series include:

Hardback   0 431 13603 3

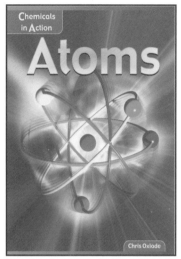

Hardback   0 431 13600 9

Hardback   0 431 13602 5

Hardback   0 431 13605 X

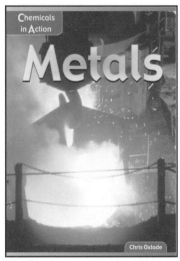

Hardback   0 431 13601 7

Hardback   0 431 13604 1

Find out about the other titles in this series on our website www.heinemann.co.uk/library